Chart Patterns Trading Bible

Forex Trading Candlestick + Price Action

BY

Jasper Bennett

Introduction

Charles Dow wrote a number of articles that were published in his opinions for The Wall Street Journal from 1900 to 1902. These articles are where chart patterns got their start. The ideas he had later grew into what is now called "Dow Theory." Technical analysis is based on Dow's observations of price movements and his understanding of trend based on the development of peaks and valleys.

They are like fractals, just like the notes Dow made and the methods used in technical analysis. This means the methods can be used for any amount of time, whether it's hourly, daily, weekly, or monthly.

You should pay attention to the following peaks and dips, or highs and lows, as you look for trends in the charts. Another important thing to know about pattern recognition is how to find the past trend based on the time period being used. You can figure out what a chart pattern means by looking at the past trend along with the current highs and lows.

The goal of this resource is to show you 50 different price trends. Every price trend has a start, a finish, and a move that is expected. For each pattern, there is a discussion of whether the pattern is positive, bearish or nondirectional. Whether it's a warning of a continuation of the trend, a reverse of the trend, or is non-directional. Also, there is an account of how volume grows during the formation of the pattern, and how to create a price projection based on the measure method for each design.

Statistical references in this book is pulled from the Encyclopedia of Chart Patterns by Thomas Bulkowski. His work reflects the most thorough study of the usefulness of chart designs to date.

1.

Broadening Bottoms

 BULLISH    REVERSAL

Directional Bias: Bullish Pattern
Type: Reversal

Pattern Description: This pattern forms at the tail end of a decline. The pattern takes on the appearance of a megaphone as the price makes a number of higher highs and lower lows throughout the formation. The pattern needs at least two highs and lows to be a proper shape.

loudness Description: The loudness should decrease through the pattern up until the breakout

Breakout Confirmation: A close above the upper trend-line on above average volume.

Measuring Technique: Measure from the highest high to the lowest low before the exit, and add that amount to the highest high for the price goal. amount to the biggest high for the price goal. year lows tend to perform better.

2.

Broadening Tops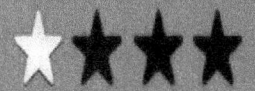

 BEARISH    REVERSAL

ROBERT HALF INTERNATIONAL, INC.

Directional Bias: Bearish Pattern
Type: Reversal

Pattern Description: At the conclusion of an upward trend, this pattern emerges. As the price develops a sequence of higher highs and lower lows throughout the formation, the pattern begins to resemble a megaphone. For the pattern to be considered genuine, it must have a minimum of two highs and lows.

loudness Description: Until the breakout, the loudness should decrease throughout the pattern.

A closure below the lower trend-line on above-average volume indicates a breakout.

Method of Measurement: To get the price goal, deduct the amount from the lowest low by measuring from the highest high to the lowest low prior to the breakout. the sum from the price target's lowest low. Year highs often have higher results.

3.

Bump-and-Run Reversal Bottoms

 BULLISH    NON-DIRECTIONAL

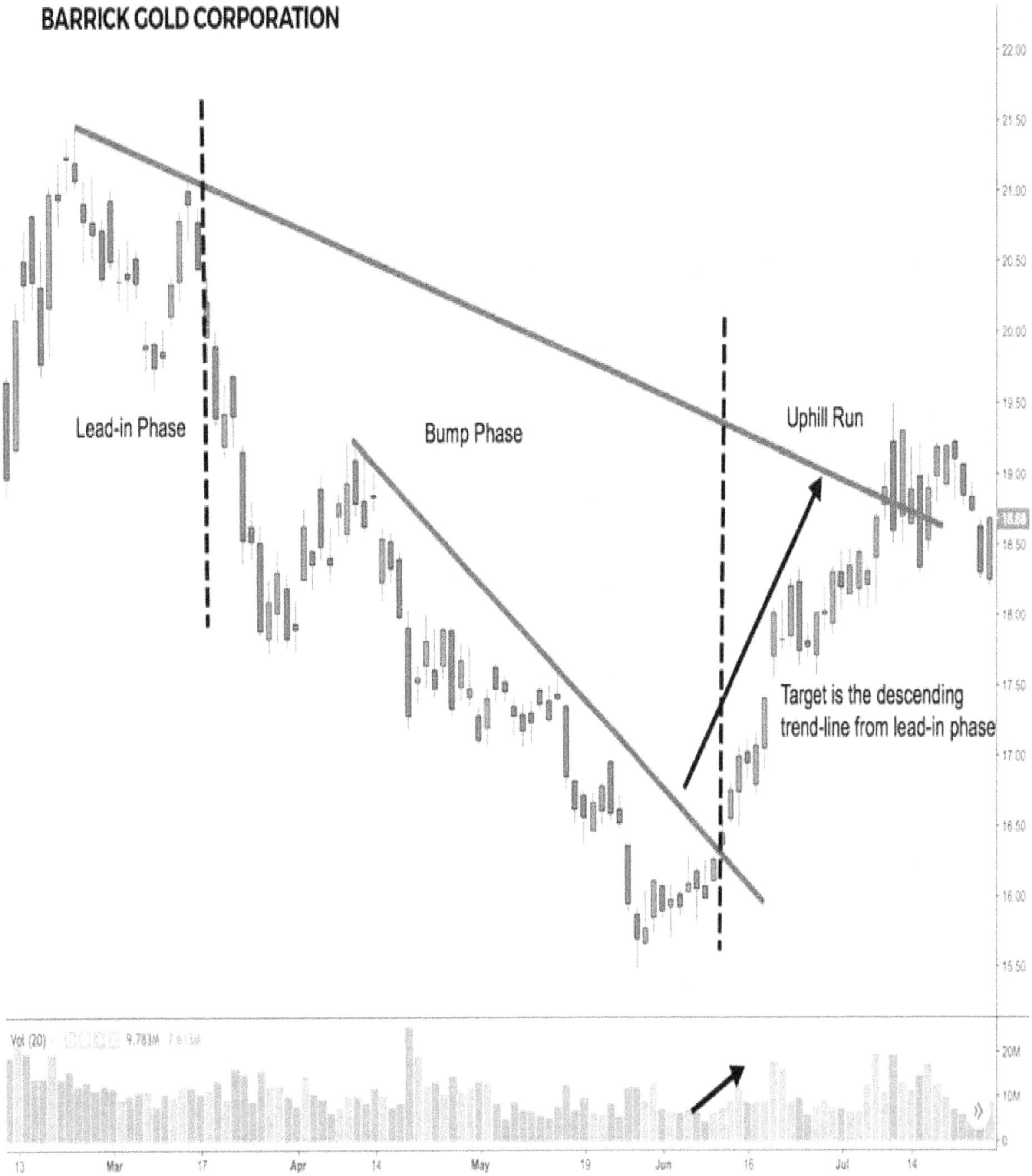

BARRICK GOLD CORPORATION

- Lead-in Phase
- Bump Phase
- Uphill Run
- Target is the descending trend-line from lead-in phase

Directional Bias: Bullish
Pattern Type: Non-Directional

design Description: This design resembles a frying pan and is divided into three stages. The lead-in, bump, and upward phases are all present. The frying pan handle represents the lead-in period prior to a more significant drop. After the decrease, the price forms a flat or rounded bottom, and the bump phase begins. The breakthrough is followed by the uphill run phase. An arithmetic chart must be utilized in order to examine this kind of formation.

Volume Description: Generally, each phase starts out loud and becomes progressively quieter as it progresses.

A closing with above-average volume that occurs during the lead-in phase above the upper trend-line established across the highs indicates a breakout.

Method of Measuring: The price objective represents the peak of the lead-in period.

Statistical Notes: A throwback to wider forms, which often perform better than smaller formations

4.

Bump-and-Run Reversal Tops

 BEARISH    NON-DIRECTIONAL

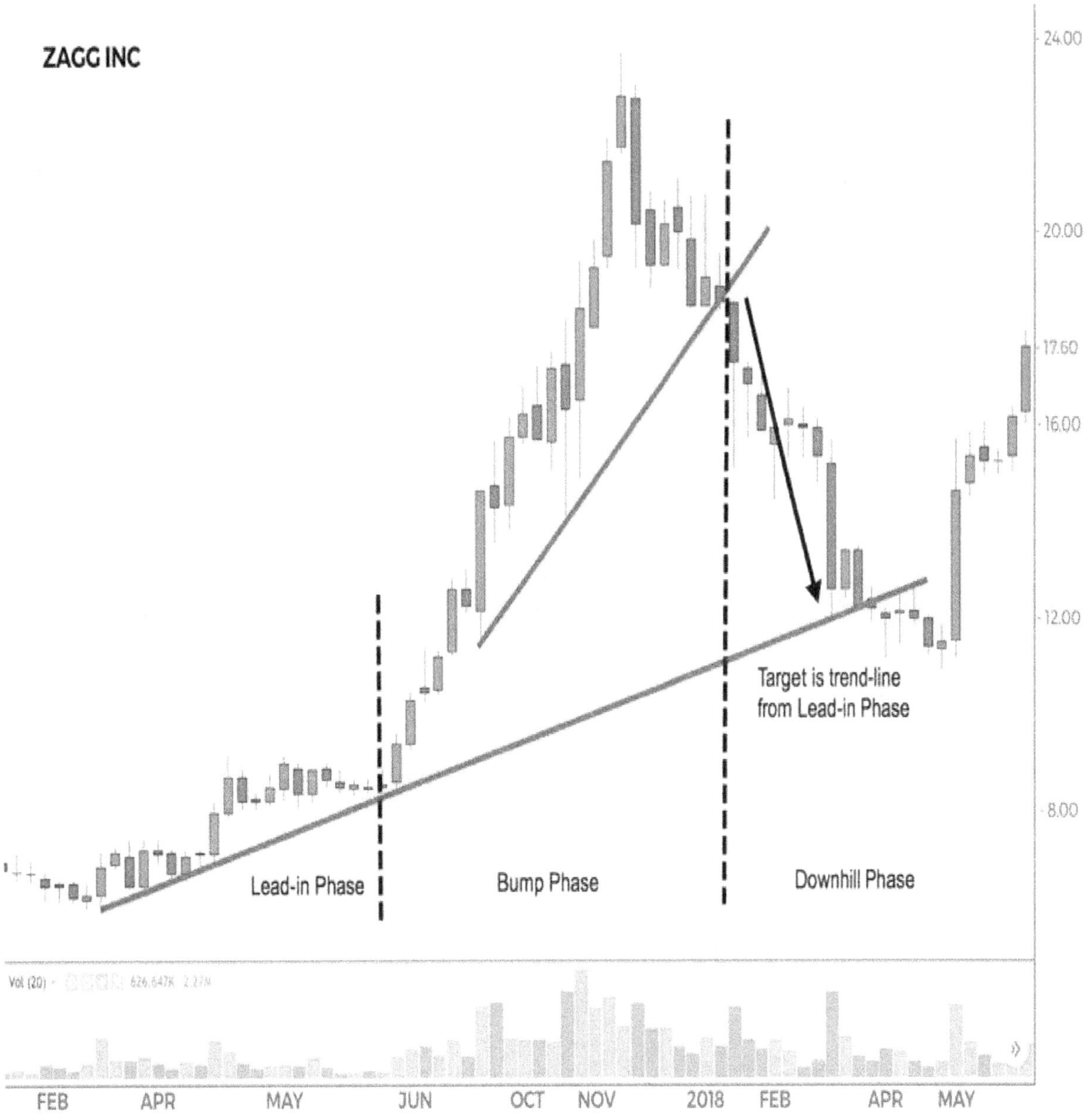

ZAGG INC

Target is trend-line from Lead-in Phase

Lead-in Phase | Bump Phase | Downhill Phase

Directional Bias: Bearish
Pattern Type: Non-Directional

Pattern Description: This design resembles a mountain range and consists of three stages. The lead-in, bump, and downward phases are all present. Comparable to a tiny range of foothills before greater mountains is the lead-in phase. The bump phase occurs after an advance when the price creates a rounded or flat top. The portion of the downhill run follows the breakout. An arithmetic chart must be utilized in order to examine this kind of formation.

Volume Description: Generally, each phase starts out loud and becomes progressively quieter as it progresses.

A closing with over normal volume that is below the lower trend-line that is drawn across the lows during the lead-in phase is a sign of a breakout.

Method of Measuring: The lead-in phase's lowest point is the price objective.

Notes on Statistics: Pullbacks and wider formations often outperform tighter forms.

5.

Cup and Handle

 BULLISH    CONTINUATION

CISCO SYSTEMS, INC.

Directional Bias: Bullish Pattern
Type: Continuation

Pattern Description: The price forms a u-shaped cup with a short handle on the right side of the pattern, which is indicative of a lengthier rise. If a daily chart is used, the cup should endure for at least seven weeks.

Volume Description: Generally, volume will follow the cup's shape, becoming higher as the left lip forms, decreasing as the cup's bottom forms, and increasing as the right lip and breakout form.

A closing above the top trend-line drawn across the handle with volume over normal indicates a breakout.

Method of Measuring: The right lip's price level is added to the price goal, which is determined by measuring the lip to the bottom of the cup.

Statistical Notes: Compared to other patterns, this one moves less strongly yet has a low failure rate. Shorter-handled patterns outperform longer-handled patterns, as do deeper cups with the left lip somewhat higher than the right.

6.

Cup and Handle (Inverted)

 BEARISH    CONTINUATION

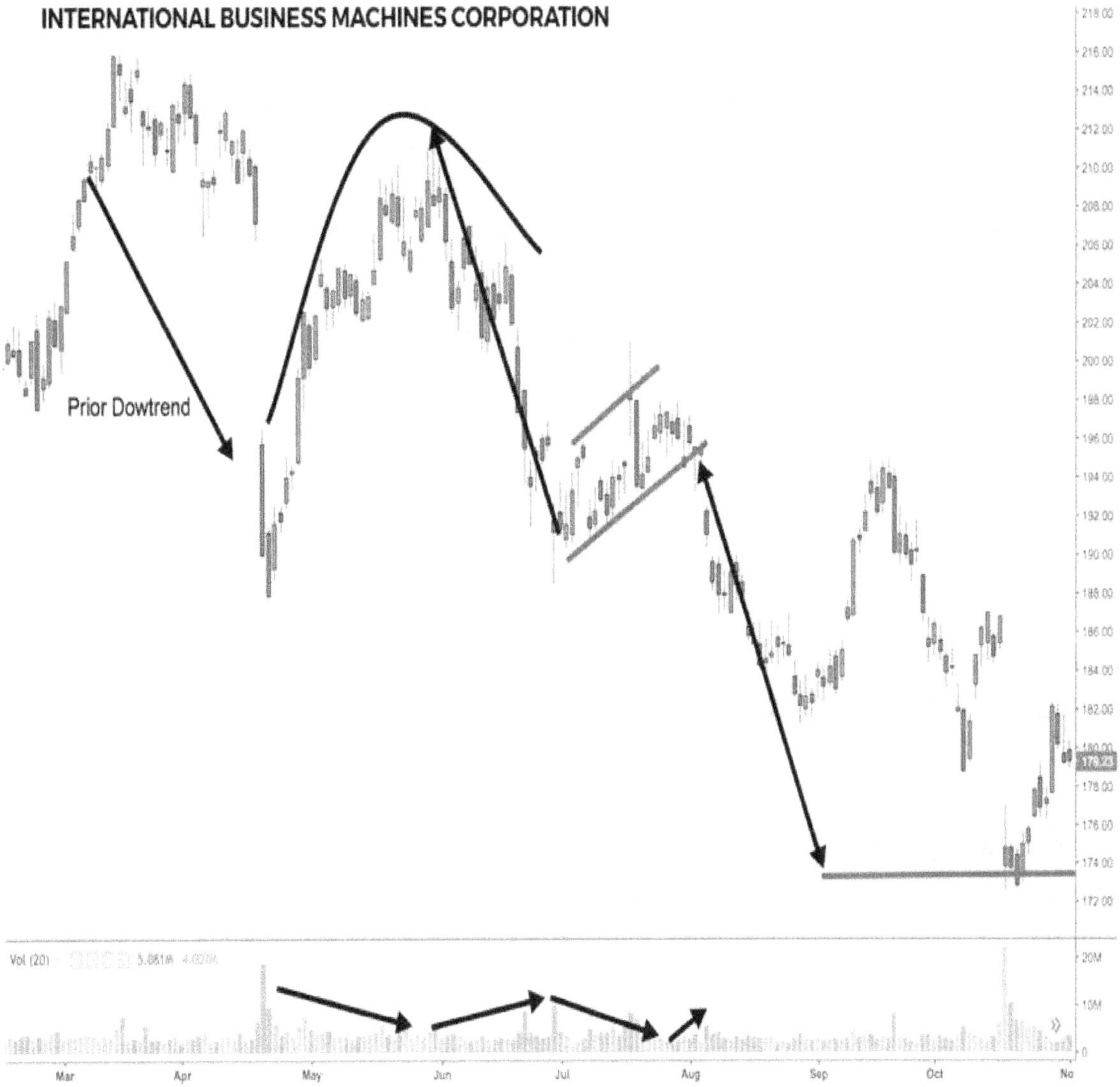

INTERNATIONAL BUSINESS MACHINES CORPORATION

Prior Downtrend

Directional Bias: Bearish Pattern
Type: Continuation

Pattern Description: The price forms an inverted u-shaped cup with a short handle on the right side of the pattern, which is indicative of a protracted downturn. If a daily chart is used, the cup should endure for at least seven weeks.

Volume Description: Volume usually follows the opposing cup shape, starting high as the left lip develops, decreasing as the cup's rounded top forms, and increasing as the right lip and breakout form.

A closing with volume over normal and below the bottom trend-line drawn across the handle indicates a breakout.

Method of Measuring: The right lip's price level is deducted from the price goal, which is determined by measuring the lip to the top of the cup.

Statistical Notes: Compared to other patterns, this one moves less strongly yet has a low failure rate. Shorter-handled patterns outperform longer-handled patterns, as do deeper cups with the left lip somewhat lower than the right.

7.

Diamond Bottoms

 BULLISH    REVERSAL

FORD MOTOR COMPANY

Directional Bias: Bullish Pattern
Type: Reversal

Pattern Description: There is a lengthier downturn surrounding this pattern. The pattern first exhibits a broadening formation with lower lows and higher highs, but it soon starts to constrict with higher lows and lower highs.

Volume Description: Volume expands on the breakout and tends to drift lower during the formation.

Confirmation of Breakout: A close with volume above normal and above the upper trend-line drawn across the downward-sloping highs.

Method of Measurement: Add the diamond's widest point measurement to the breakout level.

Notes on Statistics: Breakouts that are close to the one-year low usually perform better, while throwbacks that come after the breakout usually detract from performance. The pattern tends to revert after the goal high is reached, but it has a low failure rate and respectable upside potential. More range between highs and lows in a formation yields better results than shorter ranges.

8.

Diamond Tops

 BEARISH    REVERSAL

INVESCO QQQ TRUST

Directional Bias: Bearish Pattern
Type: Reversal

Pattern Description: There is a lengthier downturn surrounding this pattern. The pattern first exhibits a broadening formation with lower lows and higher highs, but it soon starts to constrict with higher lows and lower highs.

Volume Description: Volume expands on the breakout and tends to drift lower during the formation.

Confirmation of Breakout: A close with volume above normal and above the upper trend-line drawn across the downward-sloping highs.

Method of Measurement: Add the diamond's widest point measurement to the breakout level.

Notes on Statistics: Breakouts that are close to the one-year low usually perform better, while throwbacks that come after the breakout usually detract from performance. The pattern tends to revert after the goal high is reached, but it has a low failure rate and respectable upside potential. More range between highs and lows in a formation yields better results than shorter ranges.

9.

Double Bottom (Adam & Adam)

 BULLISH    REVERSAL

ROBERT HALF INTERNATIONAL INC.

Directional Bias: Bullish
Pattern Type: Reversal

Pattern Description: There is a lengthier downturn present when this pattern appears. The design creates two equal low points, one of which is touched by the candle for a single day and produces a v-shaped bottom.

Volume Description: Volume expands on the breakout and tends to drift lower during the formation.

A close above the upper trend-line, drawn horizontally across the high that stands between the lows with volume over average, indicates a breakout.

Method of Measurement: Add the length of time measured between the two low points and the high point to the breakout level.

Notes on Statistics: More range between highs and lows in a formation yields better results than shorter ranges.

10.

Double Bottom (Adam & Eve)

 BULLISH    REVERSAL

INTERNATIONAL BUSINESS MACHINES CORPORATION

Pattern Type: Reversal

Pattern Description: There is a lengthier downturn present when this pattern appears. Two equal lows are formed by the pattern; the first low has a v-shaped bottom where a candle from a single day touches it, and the second low has a broader bottom.

Volume Description: Volume expands on the breakout and tends to drift lower during the formation.

A close above the upper trend-line, drawn horizontally across the high that stands between the lows with volume over average, indicates a breakout.

Method of Measurement: Add the length of time measured between the two lows and the high to the breakthrough level.

Notes on Statistics: More range between highs and lows in a formation yields better results than shorter ranges..

11.

Double Bottom (Eve & Eve)

 BULLISH    REVERSAL

TWITTER, INC.

Pattern Type: Reversal

Pattern Description: There is a lengthier downturn present when this pattern appears. The design creates two equal low points, the bottom of each of which is rounded and broader.

Volume Description: Volume expands on the breakout and tends to drift lower during the formation.

A close above the upper trend-line, drawn horizontally across the high that stands between the lows with volume over average, indicates a breakout.

Method of Measurement: Add the length of time measured between the two low points and the high point to the breakout level.

Notes on Statistics: More range between highs and lows in a formation yields better results than shorter ranges.

12.

Double Tops (Adam & Adam)

 BEARISH    REVERSAL

BARRICK GOLD CORPORATION

Pattern Type: Reversal

Pattern Description: There is a lengthier uptrend surrounding this pattern. The design creates two equal high points, one of which is touched by the candle of a single day and forms a v-shaped top.

Volume Description: Volume expands on the breakout and tends to drift lower during the formation.

A closing below the lower trend-line that is horizontally drawn across the low that sits between the highs with volume that is above normal indicates a breakout.

Method of Measurement: Subtract the length of time between the two highs and the low from the breakthrough level.

Notes on Statistics: More range between highs and lows in a formation yields better results than shorter ranges.

13.

Double Tops (Adam & Eve)

 BEARISH    REVERSAL

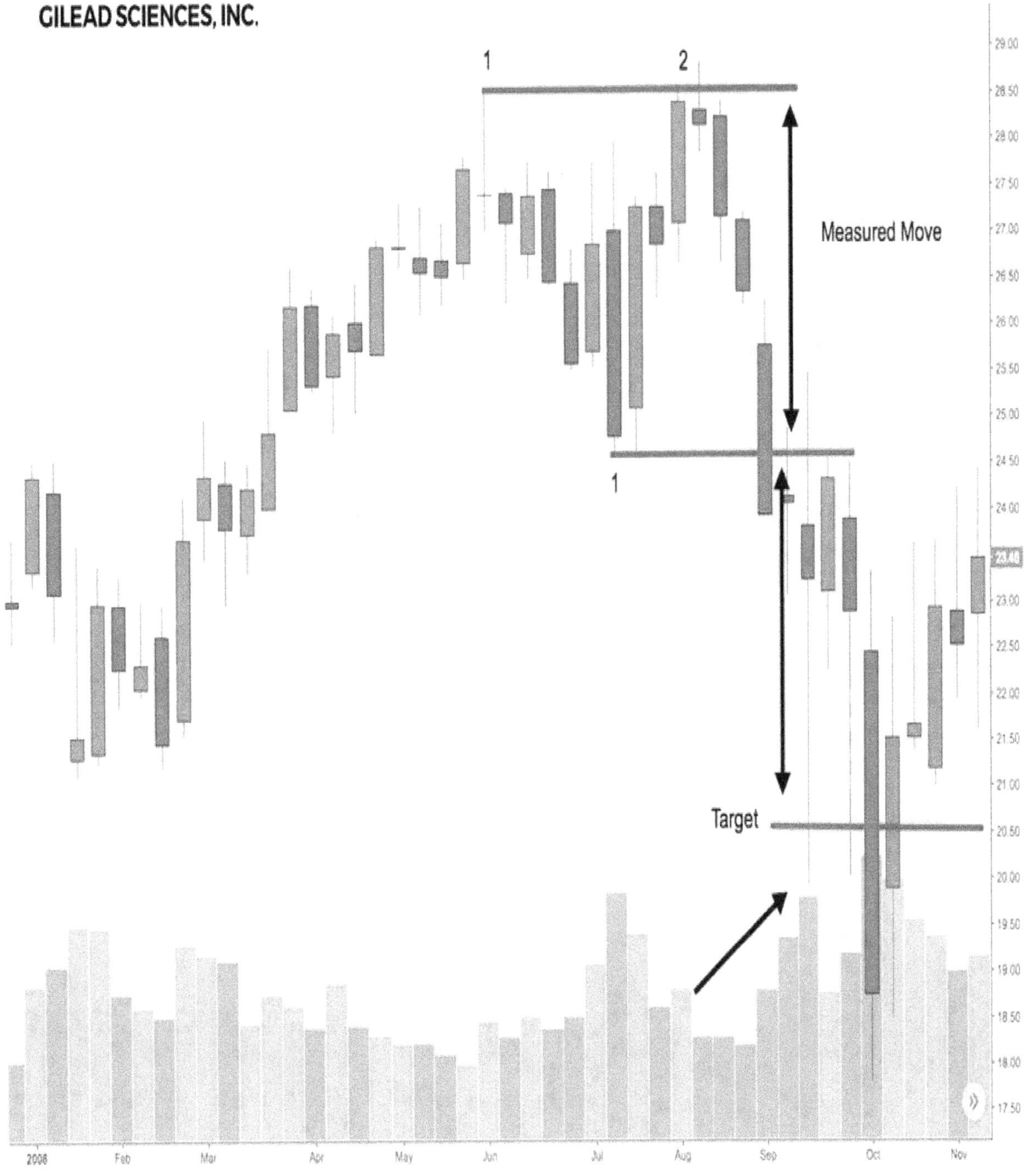

GILEAD SCIENCES, INC.

Pattern Type: Reversal

Pattern Description: There is a lengthier uptrend surrounding this pattern. Two equal highs are formed by the pattern; the first high has a v-shaped top where a candle from a single day touches it, and the second high has a wider, more rounded top.

Volume Description: Volume expands on the breakout and tends to drift lower during the formation.

A closing below the lower trend-line that is horizontally drawn across the low that sits between the highs with volume that is above normal indicates a breakout.

Method of Measuring: Deduct the distance measured from the breakout level by the length of time between the two highs and the low.

Statistical Notes: Longer range formations outperform shorter ranges in terms of high-low performance.

14.

Double Tops (Eve & Eve)

 BEARISH    REVERSAL

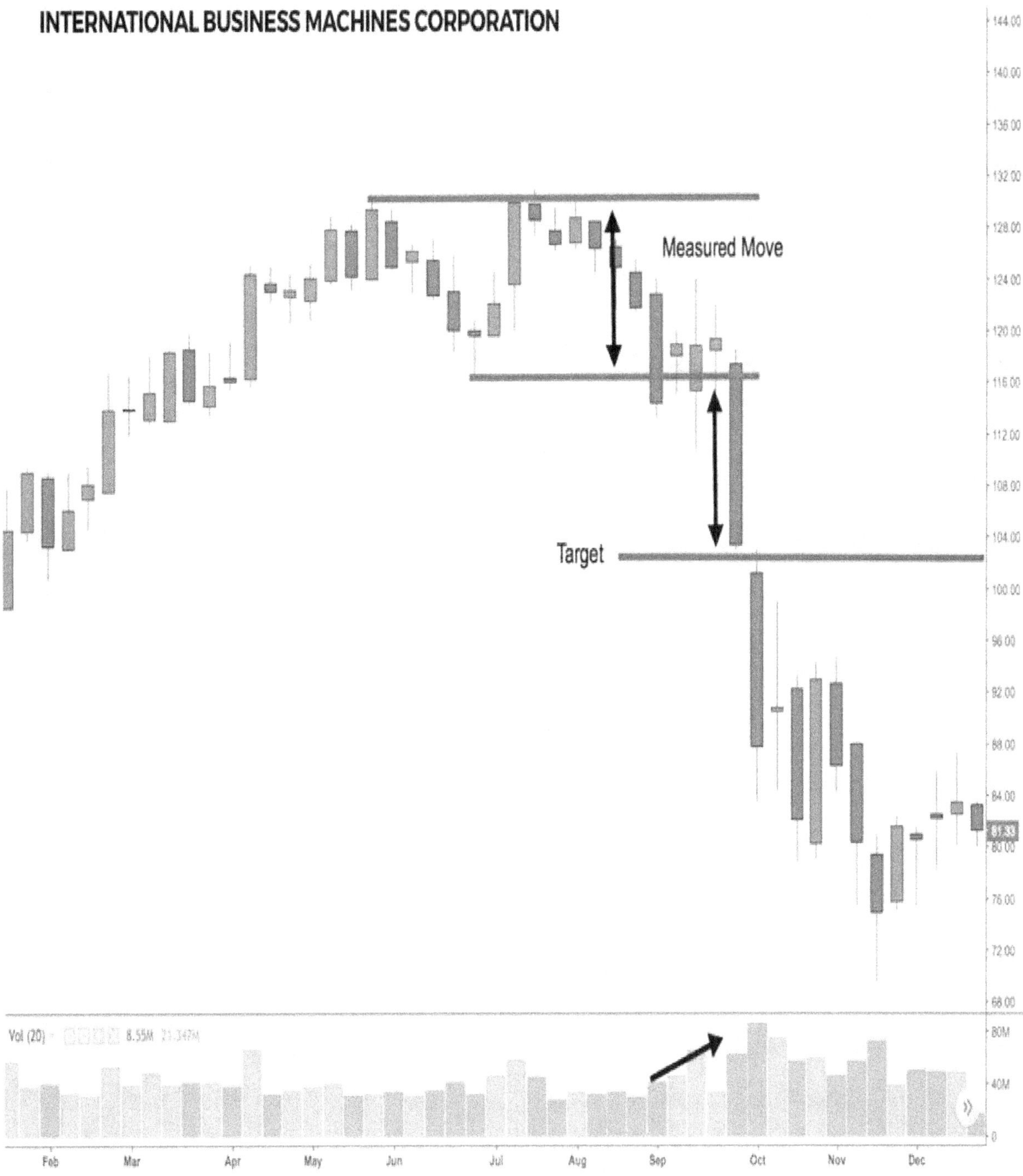

INTERNATIONAL BUSINESS MACHINES CORPORATION

Pattern Type: Reversal

Pattern Description: There is a lengthier uptrend surrounding this pattern. Each of the two equal highs in the pattern has a broader, more rounded top.

Volume Description: Volume expands on the breakout and tends to drift lower during the formation.

A closing below the lower trend-line that is horizontally drawn across the low that sits between the highs with volume that is above normal indicates a breakout.

Method of Measurement: Subtract the length of time between the two highs and the low point from the breakthrough level.

Notes on Statistics: More range between highs and lows in a formation yields better results than shorter ranges.

15.

Flags (Bullish)

 BULLISH    CONTINUATION

APPLE, INC.

Bullish Directional Bias

Typical Type: Continuation Pattern;

Description: This pattern follows a sharp, fast upward advance and appears inside the framework of a lengthier upswing. The pattern then creates a brief flag-shaped channel that slopes either horizontally or downwardly after the motion. If the pattern is charted daily, the flag section should not persist more than three to four weeks.

Volume Description: Volume expands on the breakout and tends to drift lower during the formation.

Verification of Breakout: a close with volume over normal and above the top trend-line drawn across the highs.

Method of Measuring: Determine how long the last steep move was before reaching the flag, and then add that distance to the breakout level.

Statistical Notes: Longer range formations outperform shorter ranges in terms of high-low performance. Flags without gaps often perform better than flag formations that breakout in the direction of the dominant market trend.

16.

Flags (Bearish)

 BEARISH    CONTINUATION

TWITTER, INC.

Measured Move

Target

Bearish Directional Bias

Typical Type: Continuation Pattern;

Description: This pattern follows a sharp, fast decline and appears in the context of a lengthy downtrend. After the shift, the pattern creates a brief flag-shaped channel that slopes either uphill or horizontally. If the pattern is charted daily, the flag section should not persist more than three to four weeks.

Volume Description: Volume expands on the breakout and tends to drift lower during the formation.

Verification of Breakout: a closing with volume over normal that is below the lower trend-line that is drawn across the lows.

Method of Measuring: Take a measurement of how long the last sharp move was before reaching the flag, then deduct that distance from the breakout level.

Statistical Notes: Longer range formations outperform shorter ranges in terms of high-low performance. Flags without gaps often perform better, as do flag formations that breakout in the direction of the dominant market trend. Generally speaking, bull flags outperform bear flags.

17.

Flags (High & Tight) ★★★★

 BULLISH    CONTINUATION

NETFLIX, INC.

Target
1/2 of Measured move

Measured Move

Bullish Directional Bias

Typical Type: Continuation Pattern Description: After the stock price doubles, this pattern is characterized by a narrow consolidation range that might endure for a few days or weeks.

Volume Description: Volume expands on the breakout and tends to drift lower during the formation.

A closing above the top trend-line drawn over the highs with volume above normal indicates a breakout.

Method of Measurement: The breakout level should be increased by half the length of the preceding trend, measured from low to high before the flag.

Statistical Notes: Less range results in greater formation performance than broader ranges between highs and lows. Retrospectives impair performance.

18.

Gaps (Area)

 NON-DIRECTIONAL    REVERSAL

TWITTER, INC.

Gap

Target high of day before gap

Type of Pattern: Reversal

Description of the Pattern: Area gaps are typical gaps that appear during or soon after a consolidation. The price hook that usually appears within a week to close the gap indicates an area gap.

Description of Volume: On the day of the gap, the volume usually peaks and then immediately falls.

A closing that is above or below the gap day's high or low and points in the opposite direction as the gap indicates a breakout.

Measuring Methodology: The price closing the gap and going back to the pre-gap level are the expected movements.

Statistical Notes: Regardless of the direction of the market, 90% of the time, bearish and bullish area gaps close within a week.

19.

Gaps (Breakaway)

 NON-DIRECTIONAL    CONTINUATION

INTERNATIONAL BUSINESS MACHINES CORPORATION

Pattern Type: Continuation

Pattern Description: Breakaway gaps usually appear at the beginning of a new trend after a period of consolidation. They can be bearish or bullish. The price keeps increasing after the gap to create higher highs and lows.

Volume Description: On the gap day, volume is usually much greater than the day before and stays that way for a few days. Breakout Confirmation: A price movement that breaks out of a consolidation and continues in the gap's direction after the gap day. Method of Measuring: The price is expected to move in a way that is twice as large as the move to the high gap day.

Statistical Notes: It usually takes six months or more for breakaway gaps to close. Performance is generally better for larger gaps than for smaller ones, and gaps that occur close to a 12-month high or low are better.

20.

Gaps (Continuation)

 NON-DIRECTIONAL  CONTINUATION

NETFLIX, INC.

Pattern Type: Continuation

Continuation gaps are a pattern that can be bullish or bearish and usually appear close to the center of the previous trend. The price increase is fairly steep in the gap itself. These are less frequent and usually stay open after a gap to a new high or low in the previous trend's direction.

Description of Volume: On the day of the gap, volume is normally high but not too high.

A price gap to a new high or low on increased volume in the middle of a trend is a sign of a breakout confirmation. After then, the price maintains the gap level. Method of Measurement: The projection would be the previous move to the center of the gap and then added to or removed from that middle value because the move happens in the midst of the trend.

Notes on Statistics: In bear markets, the magnitude of the bearish gap is typically greater than that of the bullish gap in bull markets.

21.

Gaps (Exhaustion)

 NON-DIRECTIONAL    REVERSAL

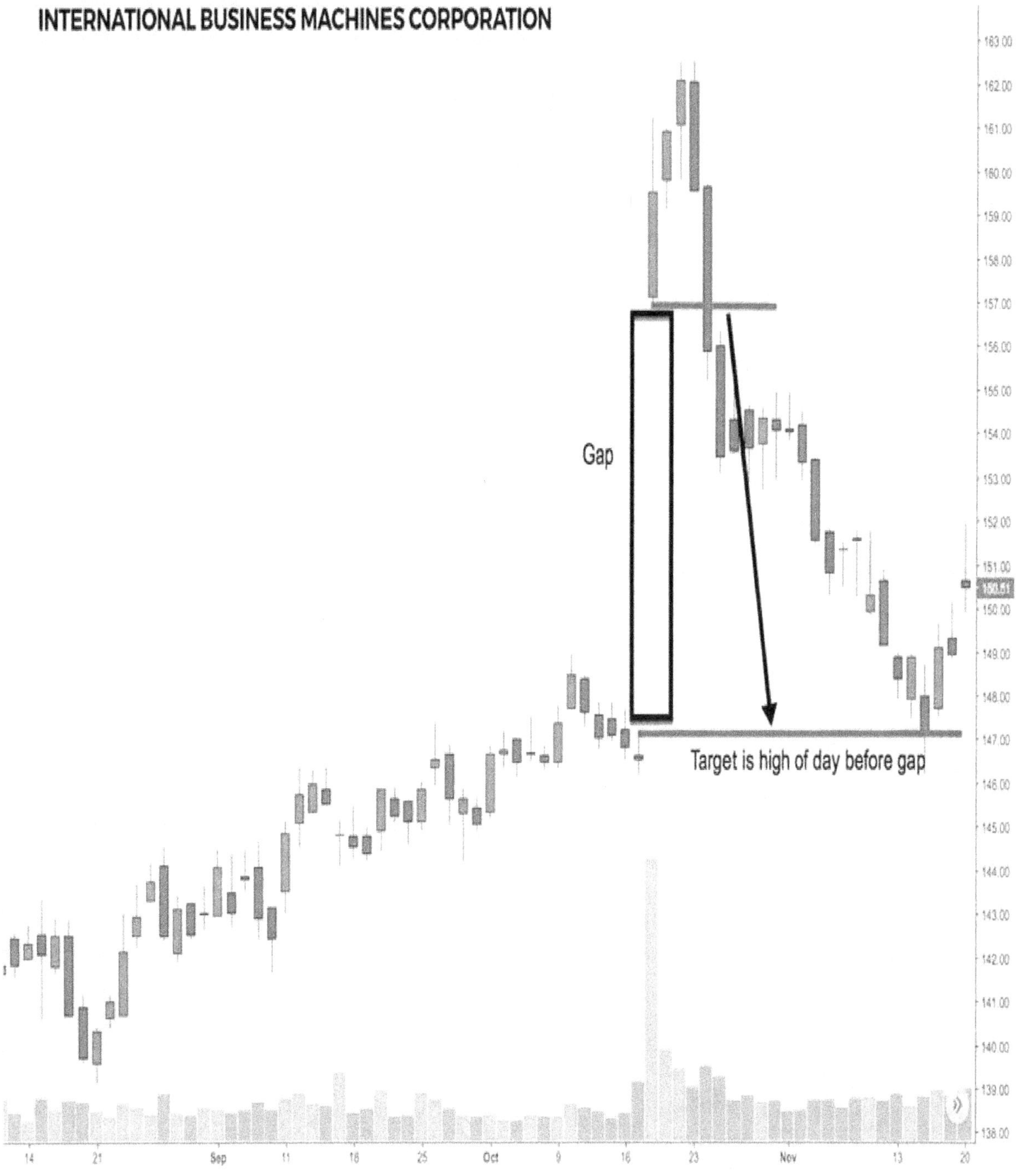

INTERNATIONAL BUSINESS MACHINES CORPORATION

Gap

Target is high of day before gap

Pattern Type: Reversal

Exhaustion gaps, which are gaps that come later in the trend and are usually bigger in size, halt for a few days after the gap before producing a new high or low.

Volume Description: Exhaustion gaps, which are the final "gasp" before a trend stops, usually happen at high volume.

A sizable gap on high volume that follows a continuation gap close to the trend's end indicates a breakout. After the gap, the price closes below the gap day's low without making a new high or low.

Method of Measuring: The day's high or low before the gap is the goal price.

Notes on Statistics: Almost two-thirds of tiredness gaps close in one week, and over 90% of gaps close after two weeks.

22.

Head & Shoulders (Inverted)

 BULLISH    REVERSAL

Type of Pattern: Reversal

The pattern is characterized by the emergence of three valleys at the bottom of a downtrend, with the middle valley, or low, generating a lower low than the other two. The trend-line that is drawn across the high points in between is called the neckline, and it should slope either horizontally or downward to the breakout region. The two shoulders and the head should develop in a somewhat symmetrical manner.

Volume Description: Volume is usually high before the first shoulder's downward motion, lowers as the price rises to complete the left shoulder, balances throughout the head's formation, and then increases as the price breaks above the neckline.

A close above the neckline and above normal volume indicates a breakout.

Method of Measurement: After calculating the length from the initial high to the head's low, add that measurement to the breakout's neckline.

23.

Head & Shoulders (Inverted Complex)

 BULLISH    REVERSAL

ALASKA AIR GROUP, INC.

Type of Pattern: Reversal

Pattern Description: This pattern is characterized by a numerous shoulders and/or head configuration and is seen near the bottom of a downturn. The trend-line that is drawn across the high points in between is called the neckline, and it should slope either horizontally or downward to the breakout region. The development of the shoulders and head(s) ought to be somewhat symmetrical.

Volume Description: During the down-moves, volume is often greater on the left shoulders, balanced toward the head or heads, and expands on the neckline breakout.

A close above the neckline and above normal volume indicates a breakout.

Method of Measurement: Calculate the length from the initial high to the head's low point, then add that measurement to the breakout's neckline.
Statistical Notes: Downsloping necklines and gaps on the breakout day typically improve performance.

24.

Head & Shoulders (Inverted Continuation)

 BULLISH    CONTINUATION

SOUTHWEST AIRLINES COMPANY

Pattern Type: Persistence

Pattern Description: This pattern is characterized by a three-valley formation that forms in the middle of an uptrend, with the center valley, or low, generating a lower low than the other two. The trend-line that is drawn across the high points in between is called the neckline, and it should slope either horizontally or downward to the breakout region. The two shoulders and the head should develop in a somewhat symmetrical manner.

Volume Description: Volume is usually high before the first shoulder's downward motion, lowers as the price rises to complete the left shoulder, balances throughout the head's formation, and then increases as the price breaks above the neckline.

A close above the neckline and above normal volume indicates a breakout.

Method of Measuring: Take a measurement of the distance from the head's low point to its initial peak, and then add that value to the breakout's neckline.

25.

Head & Shoulders

 BEARISH    REVERSAL

PROCTER & GAMBLE COMPANY

Bearish Directional Bias Typical Sort: Reversal Design This pattern is characterized by a three-peak formation near the bottom of a downtrend, with the center peak, or high, generating a higher high than the other two. The neckline is a trend line that is drawn horizontally or upwardly to the breakout region, crossing the pause lows. The two shoulders and the head should develop in a somewhat symmetrical manner.

Volume Description: Volume is balanced throughout the development of the head, tends to be high leading into the upward motion of the first shoulder, declines as the price falls completing the left shoulder, and increases as the price breaks below the neckline.

A closing below the neckline with volume over normal indicates a breakout.

Method of Measuring: Take a measurement of the distance from the head's high point to the first low point, then deduct that measurement from the breakout's neckline.

26.

Head & Shoulders (Complex)

 BEARISH    REVERSAL

DIAMOND OFFSHORE DRILLING, INC.

Bearish Directional Bias Typical Sort: Reversal Design This pattern is characterized by the emergence of numerous shoulders and/or a head at the peak of an upward trend. The neckline is a trend line that is drawn horizontally or upwardly to the breakout region, crossing the pause lows. The development of the shoulders and head(s) ought to be somewhat symmetrical.

Description of Volume: During the up-moves, volume is often greater on the left shoulders, balanced toward the head or heads, and extending on the breakout below the neckline.

A closing below the neckline with volume over normal indicates a breakout.

Method of Measurement: Subtract that much from the neckline on the breakout by measuring the distance from the initial low to the head's high point. Statistical Notes: Upsloping necklines and gaps on the breakout day typically improve performance.

27.

Horn Bottoms

 BULLISH    REVERSAL

PROCTER & GAMBLE COMPANY

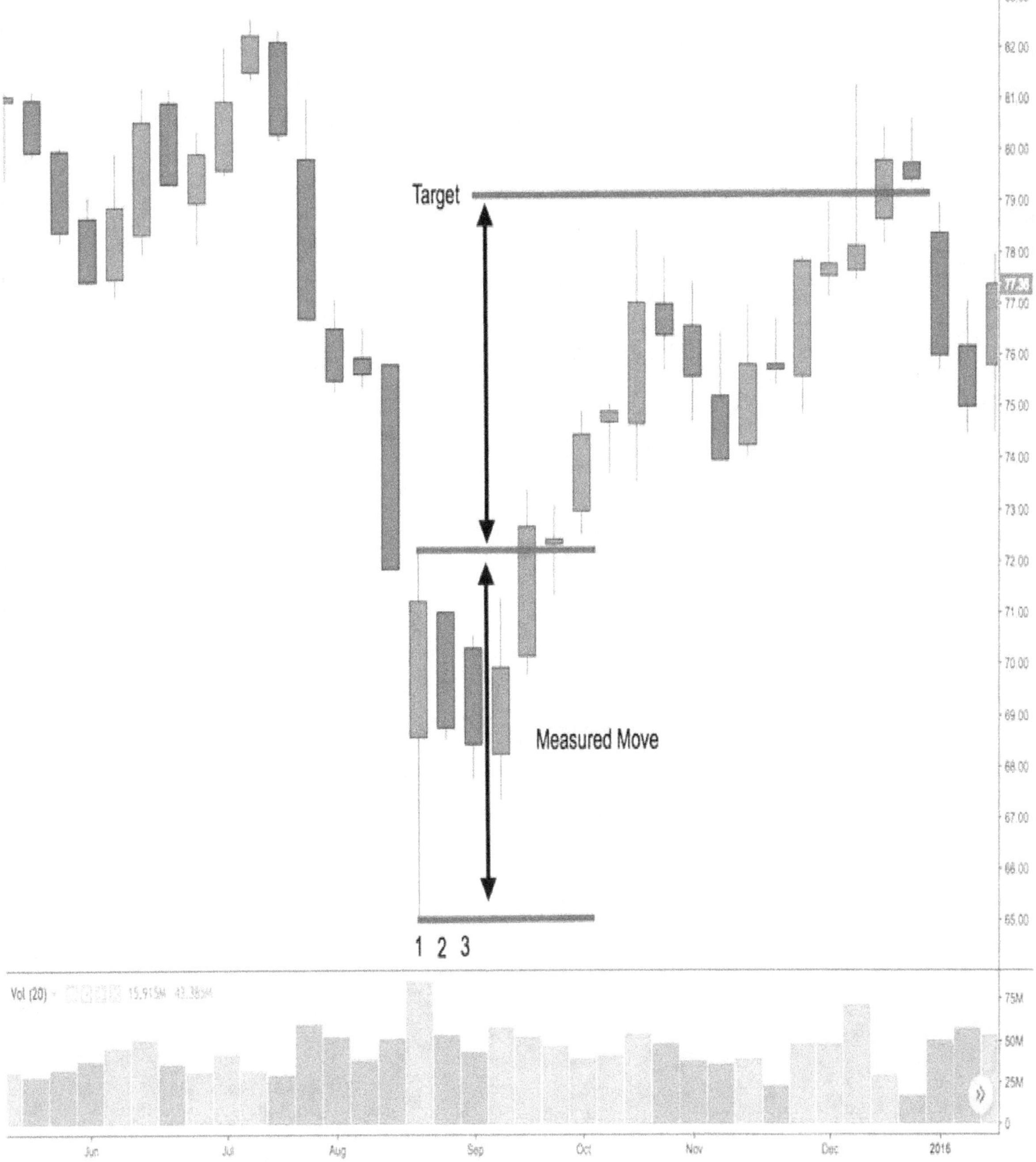

Bullish Directional Bias

Typical Type: Pattern Reversal This pattern appears as two weekly price surges that are separated by one week on a weekly chart. Compared to the previous two weeks, the center week's low should form somewhat higher.

Volume Description: During the first downward spike, volume tends to be larger, and during the second, lower.

A closing above the highest high in the three-week range indicates a breakout.

Method of Measurement: The difference between the highest high and lowest low of the three-week period is added to the highest high to determine the price goal.

Notes on Statistics: When the right spike range is inside the left spike range, horn formations function at their finest.

28.

Horn Tops

 BEARISH    REVERSAL

PROCTER & GAMBLE COMPANY

Bearish Directional Bias

Typical Type: Pattern Reversal This is a unique pattern that appears on a weekly chart and consists of two weekly intervals between rising price spikes. The middle week is supposed to form at a much lower peak than the other two.

Volume Description: During the first upward spike, volume tends to be higher, and during the second, lower.

A closing above the lowest low in the three-week range indicates a breakout.

Method of Measurement: The price objective is determined by deducting the amount from the lowest low and calculating the difference between the highest high and lowest low of the three-week timeframe. Statistical Notes: Horn formations function best when the left and right spike ranges coincide.

29.

Island Reversals

NETFLIX, INC.

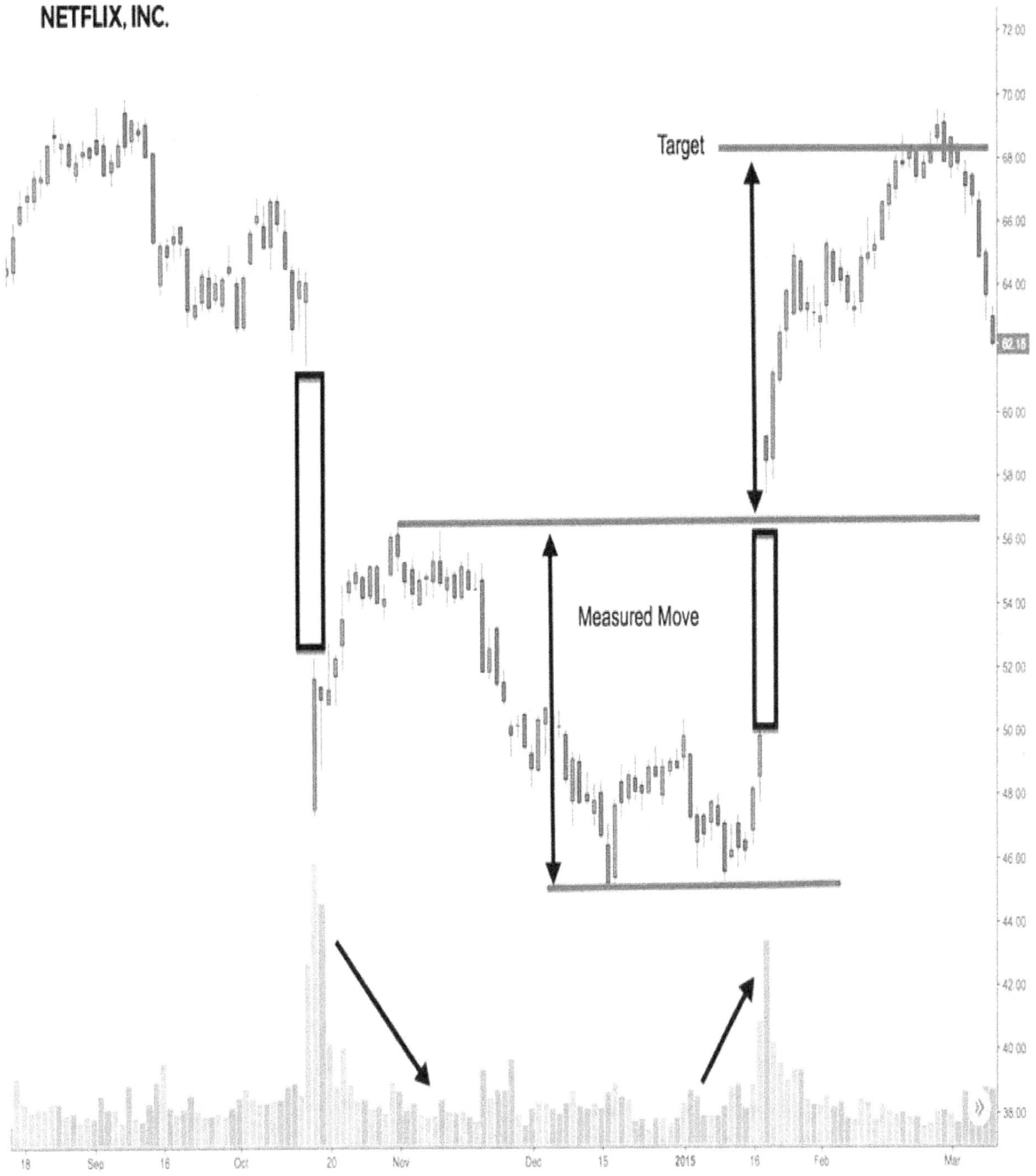

Reversal pattern is a type of non-directional pattern with directional bias.
Description: A price gap appears on the price chart, either up or down, followed by a gap that goes back to the level that preceded the first gap. An island's duration can range from one day to more than six months, with an average of slightly over a month.

Volume Description: Following the first gap's rise, volume usually decreases before expanding during the second gap.

Confirmation of Breakout: Above normal volume gap leading back to the previous level prior to the initial gap.

Measuring Method: Depending on whether the gap is bullish or bearish, take the range between the island's highest high and lowest points and add or subtract that amount from the highest high or lowest point.

Statistical Notes: Short patterns with a larger range from high to low perform best; pullbacks and throwbacks detract from performance.

30.

Pennants (Bullish)

 BULLISH    CONTINUATION

JOHNSON & JOHNSON

Bullish Directional Bias

Typical Type: Continuation Pattern; Description: This pattern follows a sharp, fast upward advance and appears inside the framework of a lengthier upswing. The pattern then creates a brief triangular formation with convergent trendlines after the move. If the pattern is followed everyday, the pennant section should not take longer than three to four weeks.

Volume Description: Volume expands on the breakout and tends to drift lower during the formation.

A closing above the top trend-line drawn over the highs with volume above normal indicates a breakout.

Method of Measuring: Determine the length of the preceding sharp move that entered the pennant by adding it to the breakout level.

Notes on Statistics: More range between highs and lows in a formation yields better results than shorter ranges. Pennant formations with gaps tend to perform better, as do pennants that breakout in the direction of the dominant market trend.

31.

Pennants (Bearish)

 BEARISH    CONTINUATION

STARBUCKS CORPORATION

Bearish Directional Bias

Typical Type: Continuation Pattern; Description: This pattern follows a sharp, fast decline and appears in the context of a lengthy downtrend. The pattern then creates a brief triangular formation with convergent trend-lines after the move. If the pattern is charted daily, the flag section should not persist more than three to four weeks.

Volume Description: Volume expands on the breakout and tends to drift lower during the formation.

A closing with above-average volume that is below the lower trend-line that is drawn across the lows indicates a breakout.

Method of Measuring: Take a measurement of the length of the preceding sharp move that entered the pennant, and deduct it from the breakout level.

Statistical Notes: Longer range formations outperform shorter ranges in terms of high-low performance. Pennant formations with gaps tend to perform better, as do pennants that breakout in the direction of the dominant market trend.

Pipe Bottoms

 BULLISH    REVERSAL

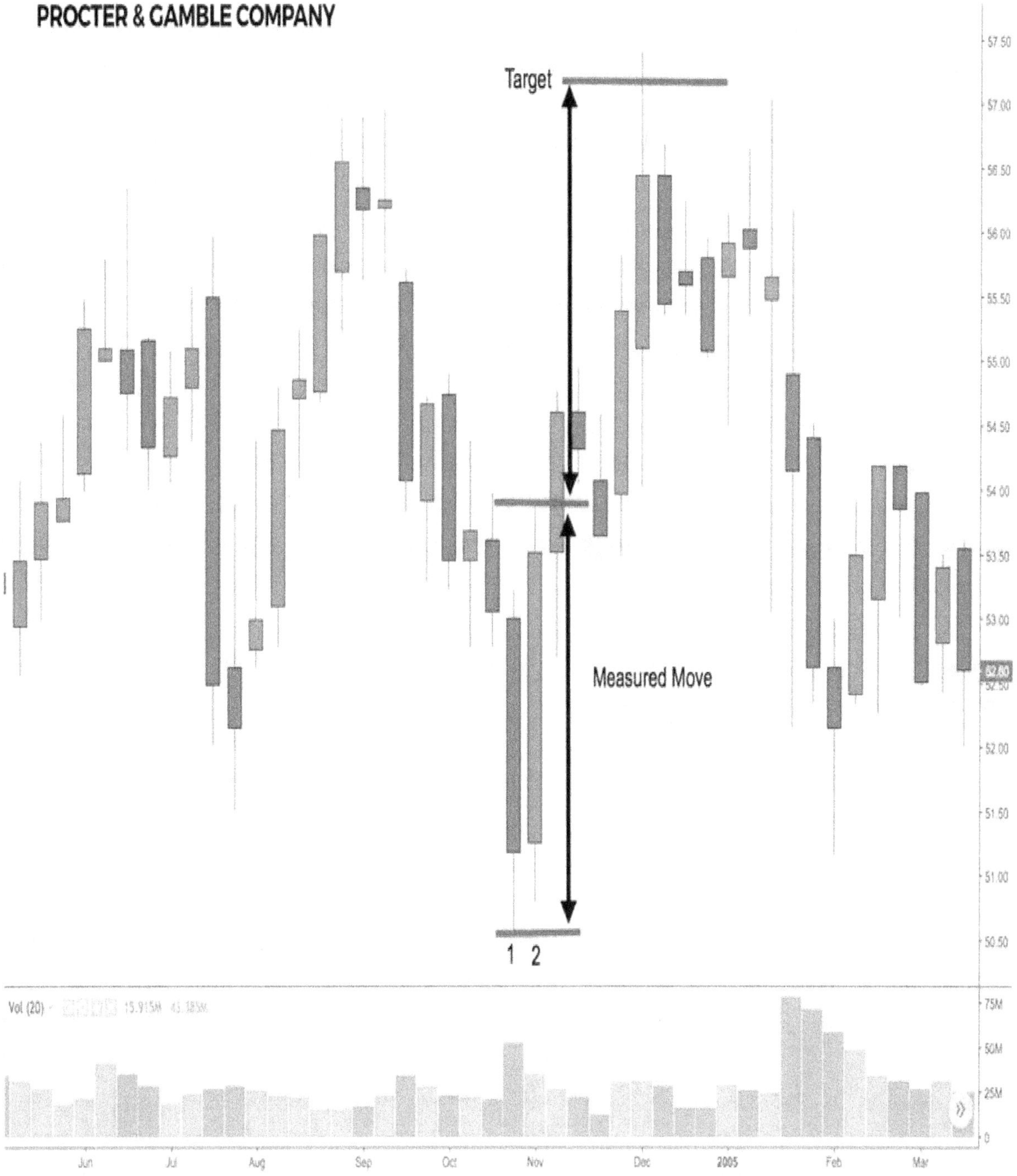

PROCTER & GAMBLE COMPANY

Bullish Directional Bias

Typical Type: Pattern Reversal Description: A weekly chart showing two successive intraweek price jumps downward.

traffic Description: Both weeks typically have above-average traffic, however the left spike typically has larger volume than the right.

A closing above the highest point of the two weekly spikes with volume above normal indicates a breakout.

Method of Measuring: Take the height of the two pipes, subtract the lowest and highest points, and add the result to the highest point.

Notes on Statistics: Performance is negatively impacted by throwbacks, and larger ranges between highs and lows outperform smaller ranges. The optimal range for a right spike is one that is within the range of a left spike.

33.

Pipe Tops

 BEARISH    REVERSAL

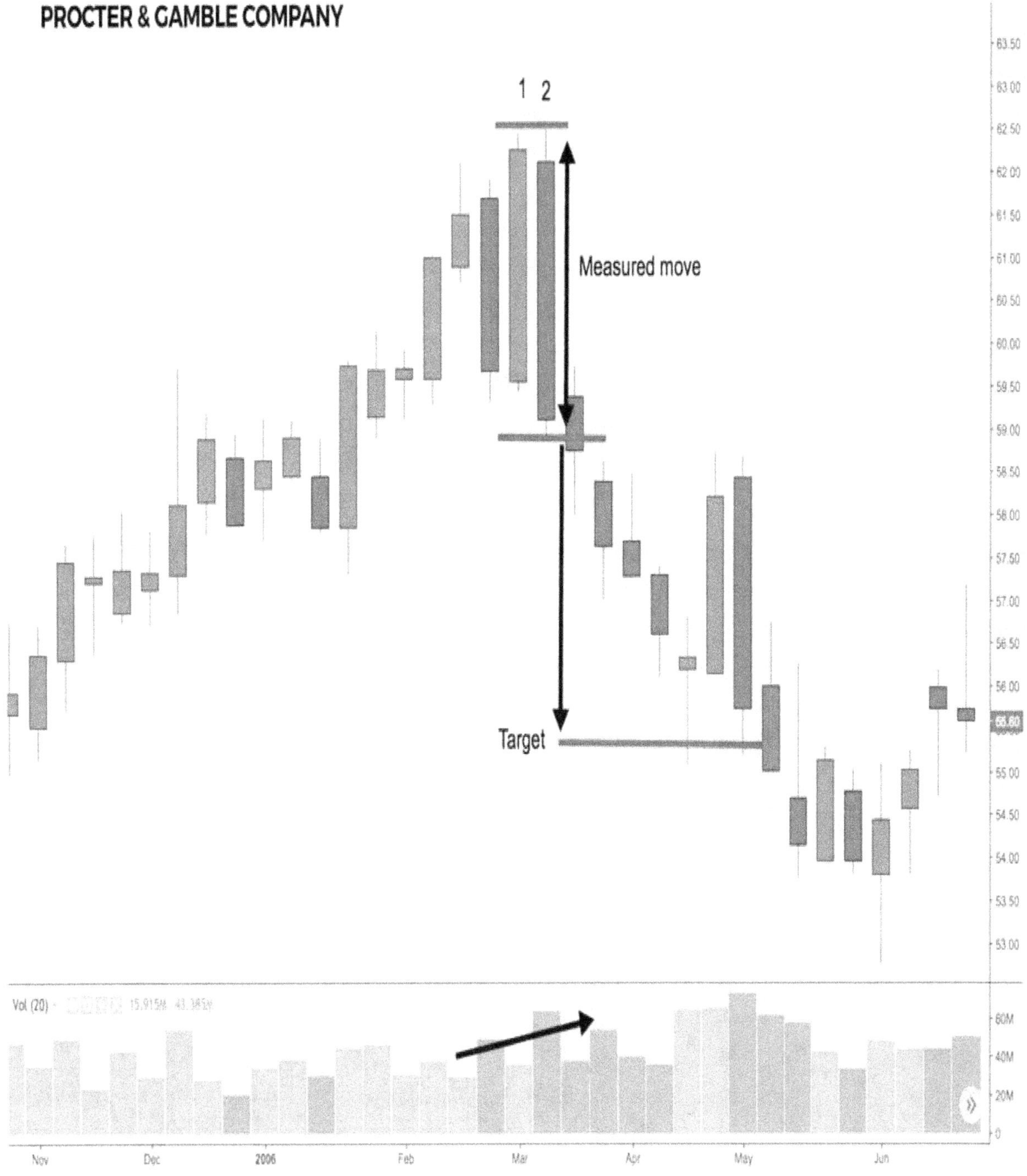

PROCTER & GAMBLE COMPANY

Bearish Directional Bias

Typical Type: Pattern Reversal Description: A weekly chart showing two straight upward intraweek price spikes.

traffic Description: Both weeks typically have above-average traffic, however the left spike typically has larger volume than the right.

A closure below the lowest low of the two weekly spikes with above normal volume is indicative of a breakout.

Method of Measuring: Take the height of the two pipes, remove the highest high from the lowest low, and then deduct that amount from the lowest low.

Statistical Notes: Larger ranges between highs and lows outperform narrower ranges, while throwbacks impede performance. The optimal range for a right spike is one that is within the range of a left spike.

34.

Rectangle Bottoms

 BULLISH    BEARISH    REVERSAL    CONTINUATION

ROBERT HALF INTERNATIONAL, INC.

Directional Preference: Positive or Negative

Pattern Type: Continuing or Reversing

Rectangles are non-directional patterns that have the potential to break out in either a bullish or bearish manner. The prior downward trend preceding the creation is what characterizes a Rectangle Bottom. When the price fluctuates between two horizontal price levels, or channels, a formation is formed.

Volume Description: Regardless of the direction in which it breaks out, volume tends to diminish during the formation and grows upon the breakout. Verification of Breakout: a little bit above or below the channel at a volume that is above typical.

Method of Measurement: Depending on the direction of the channel's break, subtract the height of the channel's highest point and lowest point, then add or remove that amount from the channel.

Notes on Statistics: Performance is negatively impacted by throwbacks, and larger ranges between highs and lows outperform smaller ranges. Rectangles with growing volume trends and no preformation rise or decline

35.

Rectangle Tops

 BULLISH    BEARISH    REVERSAL    CONTINUATION

ROBERT HALF INTERNATIONAL, INC.

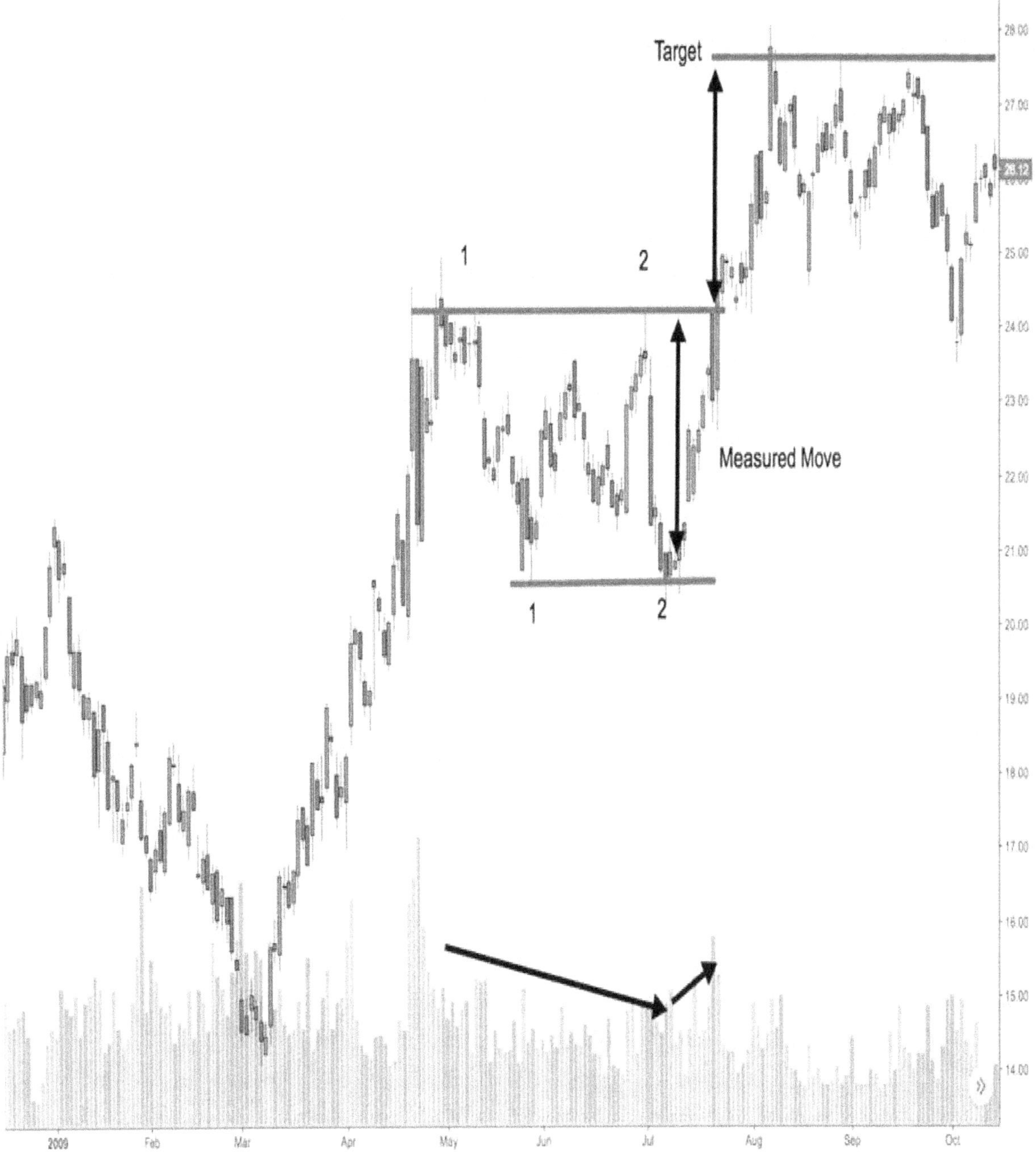

Pattern Type: Continuing or Reversing

Rectangles are non-directional patterns that have the potential to break out in either a bullish or bearish manner. The prior upsurge before the formation defines a Rectangle Top. When the price fluctuates between two horizontal price levels, or channels, a formation is formed.

Volume Description: Regardless of the direction of the breakout, volume tends to diminish throughout the formation and grows upon it. Verification of Breakout: a little bit above or below the channel at a volume that is above typical.

Method of Measurement: Depending on the direction of the channel's break, subtract the height of the channel's highest point and lowest point, then add or remove that amount from the channel.

Statistical Notes: Larger ranges between highs and lows outperform narrower ranges, while throwbacks impede performance. Rectangles with a strong volume on the breakout and a declining volume trend generally

36.

Rounding Bottoms

★★★★

 BULLISH    CONTINUATION

CLOROX COMPANY

Bullish Directional Bias

Typical Type: Pattern of Continuation An example of a Rounding Bottom pattern is one that continues the current upswing. In relation to its price, the design creates a concave or "rounded" bottom.

Volume Description: As the price rises and falls, volume usually follows suit, expanding on the breakout.

Verification of Breakout: An above-average volume near above the Rounding Bottom's lip serves as confirmation of this pattern. When the left side of the formation lacks an obvious lip, this can occasionally be challenging.

Method of Measuring: Take the height of the Rounding Bottom's highest point and lowest point, subtract them, and add the result to the breakout level. Notes on Statistics: Performance is negatively impacted by throwbacks and patterns with large high-low ranges.

37.

Rounding Tops

 BEARISH    CONTINUATION

TERADYNE, INC.

Bearish Directional Bias

Typical Type: Pattern of Continuation An example of a Rounding Top pattern is one that continues the current downward trend. The price of the design is "rounded" or concave at the top.

Volume Description: Upon breakout, volume will often expand in a u-shaped manner.

Breakout Confirmation: A closing below the Rounding Top's lip on above-average volume serves as the pattern's confirmation. When the left side of the formation lacks an obvious lip, this can occasionally be challenging.

Method of Measurement: Deduct the Rounding Top's highest high and lowest low heights, and then deduct that amount from the breakout level.
Notes on Statistics: Performance is negatively impacted by throwbacks and patterns with large high-low ranges.

38.

Scallops (Ascending)

 BEARISH    REVERSAL

NETFLIX, INC.

Bearish Directional Bias

Typical Type: Pattern Reversal A scallop develops a high, makes a slight correction, and then builds a higher high. The design resembles the letter "J."

Volume Description: As the price rises and falls, volume usually follows suit, expanding on the breakout.

Breakout Confirmation: A closing below the ascending J formation on above average volume serves as the pattern's confirmation.

Method of Measurement: Take the height of the pattern's highest high and lowest low, deduct that amount from the breakout level. Notes on Statistics: The best breakouts are those that are close to a one-year low and higher formations with increasing volume.

39.

Scallops (Inverted Ascending) ★★★★

 BULLISH  CONTINUATION

GILEAD SCIENCES, INC.

Bullish Directional Bias

Typical Type: Continuation Pattern: The price rises to a rounded high and then experiences a tiny dip. The pattern appears as an upside-down, backwards J within an uptrend.

Volume Description: Following a breakthrough, volume will often see a rising volume trend and expand.

Breakout Confirmation: A closing above the formation's rounded top on an above-average volume is the pattern's confirmation.

Method of Measurement: The height of the pattern's highest high and lowest low are subtracted, and the result is added to the breakout level.

Notes on Statistics: The finest breakouts are those that are close to one year old and taller formations with increasing volume.

40.

Scallops (Descending)

 BEARISH    CONTINUATION

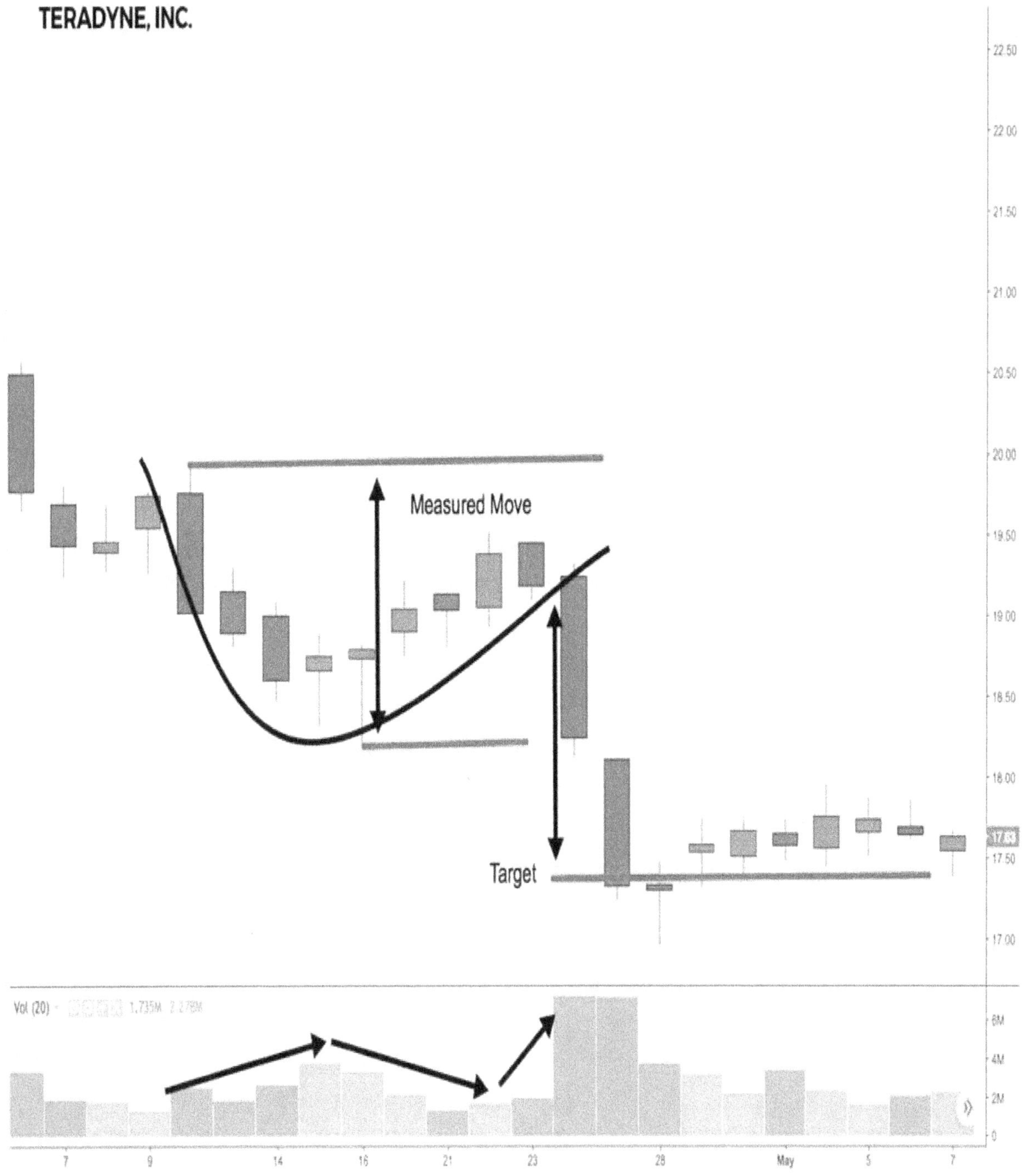

TERADYNE, INC.

Pattern Type: Continuation

The pattern known as a scallop is created when prices decline, form a rounded bottom, and then correct higher during a downtrend.

The design resembles the letter "J" written backwards.

Volume Description: When a breakout occurs, volume will often grow into a dome form.

Verification of Breakout: A closure below the ascending reverse J formation on above average volume serves as pattern confirmation.

Method of Measurement: Take the height of the pattern's highest high and lowest low, deduct that amount from the breakout level. Notes on Statistics: High volume breakout day gaps yield the best results.

41.

Scallops (Inverted Descending) ★★★★

 BEARISH    CONTINUATION

BANK OF AMERICA CORPORATION

Pattern Type: Continuation

Pattern Description: The price rises somewhat to a rounded peak and then declines more sharply, forming the appearance of an upside-down J within a downtrend.

Volume Description: Following a breakout, volume will typically expand following a u-shaped volume pattern.

Breakout Confirmation: After a brief bullish price spike, the pattern's confirmation is a closing below the upside-down J's low on above-average volume.

Method of Measuring: Take the height of the pattern's highest high and lowest low, then deduct that amount from the breakout level. Statistical Notes: Taller formations with a u-shaped volume trend and breakouts close to a one-year low perform well.

42.

Three Falling Peaks

 BEARISH    REVERSAL

GILEAD SCIENCES, INC.

Type of Pattern: Reversal

Three proportionately lower highs that usually follow an upswing are the pattern's description.

Volume Description: A u-shaped volume trend is optimal for the pattern's performance, and it grows upon the breakout.

Breakout Confirmation: A closure below the formation's lowest low on above average volume serves as the pattern's confirmation.

Method of Measuring: Take the height of the pattern's highest high and lowest low, then deduct that amount from the breakout level. The measured motion is not consistently made with this design.

Notes on Statistics: The ideal designs are short and narrow with a u-shaped volume.

43.

Three Rising Valleys

 BULLISH    REVERSAL

BANK OF AMERICA CORPORATOIN

Bullish Directional Bias

Typical Type: Pattern Reversal Typically, this pattern of three correspondingly higher lows appears near the end of a downturn.

Volume Description: During the formation phase, the pattern usually shows a dome-shaped volume trend, which extends at the breakout.

Breakout Confirmation: A closing below the formation's highest high on above average volume serves as the pattern's confirmation.

Method of Measurement: The height of the pattern's highest high and lowest low are subtracted, and the result is added to the breakout level. The measured motion is not consistently made with this design.

Statistics: Best results are achieved by breakouts close to one-year highs. U-shaped volumes with large variations between highs and lows perform well.

44.

Triangles (Ascending)

 BULLISH    CONTINUATION

GILEAD SCIENCES, INC.

Bullish Directional Bias

Typical Type: Continuation Pattern: This pattern, which forms a triangle with equal highs and increasing lows, is part of an uptrend. Two-thirds to three-quarters of the way to the triangle's apex should see the pattern burst out.

Volume Description: During the triangle formation, the volume decreases, then it increases at the breakout.

Verification of Breakout: A closure above the highs on volume above normal would confirm this trend.

Method of Measuring: Take the height of the pattern's highest points and lowest points, subtract them, and add the result to the breakout level.

Notes on Statistics: Increases volume during the breakout improve performance.

45.

Triangles (Descending)

 BEARISH    CONTINUATION

NUCOR CORPORATION

Bearish Directional Bias

Typical Type: Continuation Pattern: This pattern, which forms a triangle with equal lows and declining highs, is found within a downtrend. Two-thirds to three-quarters of the way to the triangle's apex should see the pattern burst out.

Volume Description: During the triangle formation, the volume decreases, then it increases at the breakout.

Verification of Breakout: A closure below the lows on volume over normal serves as confirmation of this pattern.

Method of Measuring: Take the height of the pattern's most high and lowest points, then deduct that amount from the breakout level.

Notes on Statistics: performs worse on pullbacks and performs better with increasing volume on the breakout.

46.

Triangles (Symmetrical)

 BULLISH    BEARISH    CONTINUATION    REVERSAL

MICROSOFT CORPORATION

Directional Preference: Positive or Negative

Type of Pattern: Persistence or Reversal

The Symmetrical Triangle pattern is non-directional and has the potential to produce a bullish or bearish breakout. This pattern is made up of triangle-shaped lower highs and higher lows. Two-thirds to three-quarters of the way to the triangle's apex should see the pattern burst out.

Volume Description: During the triangle formation, the volume decreases, then it increases at the breakout.

Verification of Breakout: A closing above or below the converging trend-lines on above average volume is indicative of the pattern's confirmation.

Method of Measurement: Depending on which way the breakout is going, deduct or add the height of the pattern's lowest low and highest high from the breakout level. Notes on Statistics: performs best in the vicinity of annual highs or lows. Performance is harmed by throwbacks and pullbacks.

47.

Triple Bottoms

 BULLISH    REVERSAL

FACEBOOK, INC.

Bullish Directional Bias

Typical Type: Pattern Reversal This pattern takes place within the framework of a more extended downward trend. Three equal lows are formed by the pattern.

Volume Description: Volume expands on the breakout and tends to drift lower during the formation.

A close above the upper trend-line, drawn horizontally between the highs in between the lows with volume over average, indicates a breakout.

Method of Measurement: Add the length of time measured between the two low points and the high point to the breakout level.

Statistical Notes: Longer range formations outperform shorter ranges in terms of high-low performance. Formations with large volume on the left bottom and decreasing volume perform better.

48.

Triple Tops

 BEARISH  REVERSAL

APPLE, INC.

Bearish Directional Bias

Typical Type: Pattern Reversal This pattern is part of a lengthier upswing that is taking place. Three equal highs are formed by the pattern.

Volume Description: Volume expands on the breakout and tends to drift lower during the formation.

Confirmation of Breakout: A closure below the lower trend-line that is horizontally drawn between the highs and the lows in between with volume that is above normal.

Method of Measuring: Deduct the distance measured from the breakout level by the length of time between the two highs and the low.

Statistical Notes: Longer range formations outperform shorter ranges in terms of high-low performance. Performance is greater for formations with decreasing volume and a lot of volume on the left top.

49.

Wedges (Falling)

 BULLISH  CONTINUATION

JOHNSON & JOHNSON

Bullish Directional Bias

Typical Type: Continuation Pattern Description: This pattern is a falling wedge formed by lower highs and lower lows that happens within an upswing. Between the highs and lows, there should be a minimum of five taps on the falling trendlines. Two-thirds to three-quarters of the way to the wedge's apex should see the pattern break out.

Volume Description: During the wedge formation, the volume decreases, and during the breakout, it increases.

Breakout Confirmation: A closure above the top descending trendline drawn across the highs on above normal volume is indicative of a breakout in this pattern. Method of Measurement: The formation's highest high is the pattern's anticipated target price. Notes on Statistics: performs worse on pullbacks and performs better with increasing volume on the breakout.

50.

Wedges (Rising)

 BEARISH  CONTINUATION

DIAMOND OFFSHORE DRILLING, INC.

Bearish Directional Bias

Typical Type: Continuation Pattern: Rising highs and lows combine to produce a rising wedge-shaped pattern that is found within a downtrend. Between the highs and lows, there should be a minimum of five taps on the rising trendlines. Two-thirds to three-quarters of the way to the triangle's apex should see the pattern burst out.

Volume Description: During the wedge formation, the volume decreases, and during the breakout, it increases.

Confirmation of Breakout: A closing below the lower ascending trendline that is drawn across the lows on above average volume serves as confirmation for this pattern. Method of Measurement: The lowest low of the formation is the expected goal price for this pattern.

Notes on Statistics: performs worse on pullbacks and performs better with increasing volume on the breakout.

www.ingramcontent.com/pod-product-compliance
Lightning Source LLC
Chambersburg PA
CBHW062112220526
45471CB00010B/3703